How To Find Your Soul mate

Find Out How To Find A Soul Mate In Amazingly Straightforward And Undiscovered Ways Without Losing Your Soul In The Process

(How To Find Your Soulmate And Begin A Successful Relationship)

Thurman Christensen

TABLE OF CONTENT

How to Develop a Successful Intimate Relationship 1
Threefold Principle 5
A Half Woman Draws A Half Man 28
How to Find Your Life's Perfect Partner 47
Are you prepared for a severe hip-hop diet? 68
The Real Story of Online Dating 76
Using dating websites online 84
Relationships to Understand 100
Why are all of my friends against you? 109
Are You Being Who You Really Are? 130
How to Discover True Love and Lasting Joy 136
Getting ready to meet your soul match 147

HOW TO DEVELOP A SUCCESSFUL INTIMATE RELATIONSHIP

In these days of social media, it appears simple to "connect" with others, communicate wishes and dreams, profile photos, and background details. Despite these "easy" ways to "meet" people, you can still find yourself alone and want to have a close connection with someone special. Unfortunately, you are unable to fulfill this desire.

So, what do you think? Is it true that there aren't enough "others" in the pool of singles to choose from, after all? Or may there be something in you that prevents you from finding the intimate connection you so desperately want?

Well, it is "comfortable" and simple to believe that the "special one" has not yet been found. It is convenient to believe that "many out there" are just inappropriate for you.

But is it really the case? Could it perhaps be that something about you prevents you from finding "the one and only" in the end? If that's the case, is there anything you can do to address it?

Yes, there is a lot you can do about it. You need to come to know yourself better, to understand what is getting in the way of you discovering and cultivating a healthy intimacy, and to recognize what may have contributed to the damage you have done to your relationships up to this point. This "a lot" may be summed up in one line.

You can refer to this process as "cognitive therapy" that you undertake on your own to complete, or you can refer to it as "becoming aware," which will bring to the surface any thinking and behavioral patterns that may have prevented you from having a successful relationship up until this point.

What it all boils down to is: are you really eager to learn how you relate to people; What are your needs? How can you be getting in the way of developing a satisfying relationship? And lastly, how do you go about being aware of the many ways that you may have harmed your relationships up until now without realizing it and how to alter things for the better?

The game's name is "taking responsibility." Accepting responsibility for your mistakes, as well as for being self-aware and taking the required action to change whatever has to be changed.

Being responsible and self-aware doesn't always mean you have to stop "meeting" people online. The opposite may even be true: as you work to become conscious, every person you "meet" has the potential to reflect something back to you and so "tell" you something about yourself. You can see the projections you "throw" at each and every individual you encounter. the motivates you to project those aspects and parts of yourself onto them? Is it jealousy? Stubbornness? Stinginess? Shyness? Vulnerability? Insecurity?

The more self-aware you become, the more you'll start to see yourself "as if from the side" and realize how you act and think. As a result, you'll realize what needs to change in your thinking, attitudes, and behaviors for you to finally find and cultivate the successful intimate relationship you long for.

THREEFOLD PRINCIPLE

3. The Manifesting Magic series' books are always intended to be succinct yet effective. Instead of trying to fluff out the book as a typical author would, I've chosen to offer you clear, doable advice that you can take to heart and use to your daily life. In the last portion of Manifesting Magical Relationships, I want to address an issue that many people have with what they have read so far.
4. The idea that you receive what you give and that, if you want more love, you should offer more love is one that most people can understand. When individuals are receiving the reverse of what they are giving, this concept becomes difficult to apply. For instance, even if you have high ideals against adultery and are a very faithful person, you often find yourself with a cheating spouse. Or, in the most severe case, it's possible that you often find yourself in

emotionally or physically violent relationships. Given your circumstances, it would be entirely acceptable if you disagreed with any portions of this book.
5. I want you to know that even if you are not reciprocating the unfavorable behavior you are experiencing, you are still bringing it into your life. Just keep in mind what I mentioned about the magical ray cannon (which lacked a safety switch). Whatever you fire that gun at will materialize, and there are no safeguards to prevent you from having absolutely terrible results. The issue is that you are unable to consciously reach the area of your being where this magical manifestation tool is located. Even while it may seem unfair or annoying at first, it is really for the best that you cannot access this weapon of mass devastation or state of pleasure. Every second of every day, your subconscious is shooting the ray gun under direct control, causing things in your life that it thinks you want to happen. You may wonder why this part of you is so blind to the fact that many of

the things it brings you are bringing you suffering and anguish. However, the subconscious cannot evaluate or dispute the instructions being transmitted to it. You are constructing the reality "I am fat" if, for the most of your life, you have looked in the mirror and thought to yourself, "Boy, you are fat." The directive is received by your subconscious, which follows it without passing judgment. Guess what scenario your subconscious would choose to be the reality you want replicated if you feel that all employers are bastards and that every boss you've ever had treated you with little respect?

6. Don't misinterpret this aspect of your subconscious and don't criticize it. Without it, you would already be dead. In addition to knowing how to get you across a busy road, what to do when you fall into water, and how to act on the edge of a tall building, it has successfully designed programs to prevent you from touching the hot stove. Millions of programs that your subconscious mind has created over the years are active without your knowledge. Think about

crossing the street when a speeding car was headed directly in your direction. Your subconscious has already evaluated the danger and loaded the precise survival software to get you out of harm's path in less than a second. Do you want the program to start right away or should you be prompted for approval?

7. There must be certain motifs in your life that keep coming up. Events and circumstances that keep occurring to you again. Or maybe you have seen self-destructive behaviors in your friends' and family members' life. My buddy Brian has been repeating the same dating program for the last thirty years. Since I first got to know Brian about three decades ago, Brian has been frantically searching for someone to love.
8. The relationship program that Brian uses, which I have seen performed hundreds of times over the last thirty years, is shown here.
9. A girl is met by Brian.
10. Brian has a girl's like.

11. Brian experiences love nearly immediately.
12. Girl is alarmed by how quickly he moves.
13. Girl begins to regress in an effort to slow him down.
14. When Brian notices her desirability, his desire grows.
15. In an effort to calm her fears, Brian does the exact opposite of what she needs.
16. Girl breaks up the romance.
17. Brian feels heartbroken and finds it hard to accept that she wasn't "the one."
18. Restart by going back to the beginning.
19. You have no idea how many times I have seen this procedure execute from start to finish. My heart somewhat breaks each time Brian calls me and begins the conversation with, "Hey Craig, I have met the most amazing woman." In that instant, I know we are about to embark on a ten-step journey that will entail several talks like to those from Groundhog Day and will ultimately

lead to me consoling a grieving Brian after yet another traumatic breakup. Of course, he could eventually stumble across the real lady of his dreams, but this won't happen until he overturns the program that has been operating in the background of his mind.

20.
21. Brian's major issue is that he is unaware of the program's existence. I've told him several times, but he refuses to believe it's possible, and he always begins a new relationship by saying, "I know I've said this before, but I know that with [INSERT WOMAN'S NAME] it will be different." The main issue you have is that most of your own detrimental habits go unnoticed by you. Even worse, even if you were aware of them, there isn't much you could do deliberately to get rid of them (because you can't get to where they are kept). assume for a moment that I take up my mobile phone, call you right now, and yell, "Help, I've locked myself out of my house," just to show you what I mean. Then, assume that my battery dies, and

the call disconnects. You don't know where I live, and even if you did, you wouldn't have a key to enter the door, so there is no way you can help with this issue. You would be spending your time trying to fight the bad programs out of your mind, and I would be wasting my time begging you for assistance.

22.
23. So how do you handle issues that are located somewhere you can't go to? If you can't identify the specific part of your mind that is at fault, you must purge it all. The idea of embracing silence and allowing a power higher than yourself to restore the parts of your existence that your ego has destroyed is what is meant by spiritual cleansing. There are several techniques for doing this, including drumming and chanting activities, yoga, and meditation. Ho'opono'pono, however, is the most potently effective treatment I have ever discovered.
24. If you are unaware of the Ho'oponopono ancient Hawaiian healing

technique, please believe me when I say that I am about to transform your life.
25. The traditional Hawaiian practice of acceptance, forgiveness, and appreciation is known as ho'oponopono. This is without a doubt the most significant piece of information I have ever acquired. Accepting responsibility for everything in your life is the first step in this really simple yet completely effective technique. I really mean everything when I say everything! You must entirely give up the idea of assigning blame and abandon the tendency to think that certain problems are "someone else's problem" if you want to significantly improve your life. The first lesson of this deep insight is that you become responsible for something when you become aware of it. Regardless of whether it affects you directly or simply someone you know, repairing it is your responsibility, even if it's not your fault.
26. At first, it's a bit difficult to embrace this idea since your ego tries to defend you from the allegations of guilt.

Additionally, it doesn't give a damn about other people's health and doesn't want you to expend time and energy making anybody else's life better than your own. The ego is irrational, as it always is, and once you learn to disregard it and accept full responsibility for everything in your life, then wonderful things will begin to happen to you.

27. What does "completely responsible" mean?
28. It denotes your understanding that you are not separate from others and that whatever that happens to someone else must also happen to you. Everything you become aware of is something you created, and only you have the power to either be grateful for it or remove it if it is hurting anybody (including yourself). Your subconscious and soul's divine force has produced everything in your life that you categorize as good or negative. In essence, since you are a part of God, you possess God's power, but unfortunately, your ego gets in the way and creates significant issues. It is like to

handing a 12-year-old the keys to a Lamborghini capable of 200 mph and expecting him not to wreck it.
29. The ego unintentionally transmits false programming to the subconscious as it tries continuously to experience pleasure and avoid anxiety. This aspect of you just executes the software without passing judgment or asking any probing questions, and before you realize it, a mountain of sorrow has been delivered into your life. That you would cause yourself such suffering seems completely absurd, so you begin seeking for someone else to blame. Everything in your life and the lives of others around you is governed by this idea.
30. You must acknowledge that you are to blame for the problem if you are overweight and dissatisfied with the size and form of your body. No longer can you point the blame upon your parents, huge bones, heredity, or the nearby doughnut store where you work.
31.
32. It is your obligation if your buddy is suffering financial difficulties. The fact

that you are aware of it proves that it exists inside you, even if I don't intend for you to bail her out or beat yourself up and feel as terrible as they do.
33.
34. Your boss is being a jerk and making your job at the company unbearable. Your accountability for his actions is clear.
35. I'll say it again: Taking full responsibility does not make everything that happened your fault. The moment we stop playing the blame game, the idea of fault is no longer important. The idea that you created the world could strike some people as absurd or just figurative. But if you pay close attention, you'll see that anything you refer to as the world and believe it to be is really a projection of your own mind.
36. You may see this if you attend a party. In the same setting, with the same people, food, drink, music, and ambience, some will have fun while others will be bored, some will be too exuberant while others will be gloomy,

and some individuals will chat while others will remain quiet.

37. Everybody's "out there" seems to be the same, but if their brains were connected to machines, it would quickly become apparent how various parts of the brain come to life and how each individual has a unique perspective. Even if they seem to share it, their inner world and feelings are not the same as what is "out there" for them.

38. Through the book "Zero Limits," which he co-wrote with a pretty strange clinical psychologist by the name of Dr. Hew Len, Joe Vitale first exposed me to this ancient knowledge.

39. There used to be a specialized ward and clinic for offenders with mental illnesses at Hawaii's Hawaii State Hospital more than thirty years ago. People who had committed exceptionally serious crimes were sent there, either because they had a severe mental illness or because a mental health evaluation was necessary to determine if they were mentally fit to stand trial. They had committed rape,

abduction, murder, and other crimes. A nurse who worked there during those times said that the environment was so desolate that not even paint could adhere to the walls; everything was rotting, scary, and unpleasant. There was seldom a day that went by without a patient-prisoner assaulting another inmate or a staff member.

40. Even though they were all constantly chained, the staff members were so terrified that they would huddle against the walls if they spotted a prisoner walking toward them in a hallway. The convicts' constant threat-making mentality prevented them from ever being taken outdoors to obtain some fresh air. Staff shortages were a recurring problem. The majority of the time, nurses, wardens, and other staff members would like to be off work due to a hazardous and depressing situation.

41. Dr. Stanley Hew Len, a recently hired clinical psychologist, showed up to the ward one day. The nurses rolled their eyes, preparing for one more person who would pester them with

fresh ideas for how to improve the terrible situation before leaving as soon as things became uncomfortable, typically around a month later. But that's not what this new doctor would do. He really didn't seem to be doing anything special; he simply kept coming in and smiling and being happy in a very natural manner. He didn't even consistently arrive at the crack of dawn. He would sometimes inquire for the detainees' files.

42. But he never made an attempt to meet them in person. He reportedly merely sat in an office, perused their records, and spoke to staff employees who showed interest in a strange practice known as Ho'oponopono. Things at the hospital began to alter gradually. The atmosphere improved when someone eventually tried to paint those walls again and they actually remained painted. Some tennis courts were renovated, the grounds began to be maintained, and some convicts who had previously been prohibited from going outside began to play tennis with the

staff. Other convicts could be released from their chains or get less potent pharmaceuticals. More and more people were able to leave the hospital unfettered and without bothering the staff.

43. By the time all was said and done, the crew was no longer on sick leave. Prisoners were progressively freed. Dr. Hew Len spent almost four years there. Only a few prisoners were left in the end, and they were finally transferred to other facilities, forcing the closure of the clinic for offenders with mental illnesses.

44. Even if there are seminars where you may learn all the many tips and techniques for doing the ho 'oponopono ritual, according to Joe Vitale, Dr. Hew Len just employs the most basic formulae. You simply need to say: "I'm sorry," "Please forgive me," "Thank you," and "I love you" when anything goes wrong—and they always do.

45. Look for Joe Vitale's book Zero Limits if you want to learn more about the history and supporting documentation of Ho'oponopono. Joe

goes into great depth about how this wonderful, down-through-the-ages technique really works miracles.
46. If you download one of my subconscious reprogramming songs, you'll see that every recording has definite indications of this technique. Although I don't often mention Ho'oponopono, you can count on hearing the phrases "I'm sorry, please forgive me, thank you, and I love you" throughout the hypnosis songs.
47.
48. You may locate a subattraction TM download on the internet at craigbeck.com that specifically addresses your goal or issue, whether you are merely trying to quit smoking or are hoping to attract the person of your dreams into your life.
49.
50. Simply accepting your flaws and asking for forgiveness will allow you to start creating the life of your dreams. I don't mean you have to apologize in the sense of a Catholic confessional, where you put a tremendous amount of

humiliation on your own shoulders. Your acceptance and apologies are only a way of saying that you realize there is something artificial within of you that is impeding the flow of divinity; they do nothing. Since these feelings are exclusively human and have no bearing on a flawless source of creation, God/Source/The Universe is not disappointed in you, irritated with you, or ashamed of you. Your conscious mind is unable to alter the negative programming or false ideas that are present in your subconscious because it lacks the necessary strength.

51.
52. Only the universe has the power to correct the patterns that are out of alignment, and by making this apology, you enable the process to start. You can't even start looking for hidden beliefs since you have no idea what they are. Accept that they exist, that you are entirely responsible for them, and that you are sorry that they exist at all. Request forgiveness from the universe, source, divinity, God, or whatever name

you like. Ask that it be removed and replaced with an emptiness that can only be filled with the divine white light.

53.

54. Your life will start to feel like a vase full of water as you start this process; when the vase is devoid of happiness and love, you feel cut off from the source. When the vase is completely filled, the contents quickly spoil like water in a still lake. The vase's contents must flow continuously for perfection to exist in life. You make room for more love to enter when you pour out that vase of love into other people's lives.

55.

56. There will always be an abundance if you have the capacity to accept what is ready and wanting to come into your life. Create the space each day for more love to flow into your life by giving as much as you can.

57. Let's review the Manifesting Magic connection tenets:

58.

59. Recognize that what you perceive is not accurate. Rarely do people behave

in such a hurtful manner against you. With the tools we have, we are all doing our best. We are all attempting to flee from or toward pain or pleasure.
60. Be cautious what you put out there because it will return right back at you because life is like a giant boomerang.
61. Everything that happens in your life is entirely your fault. You created and are the manifestor of this existence. You have the ability to fix the damaged programs and swap them out for new, "life-enhancing" ones if there are parts of it (or particular connections) that you are dissatisfied with.
62.
63. What Have I Been Doing Recently for Me?
64.
65. That chapter title strikes you as being somewhat self-centered, don't you think? You are not to fault if you believe that. We are taught to put other people's needs ahead of our own as we grow up. And there is nothing wrong with it at all. Serving others is a wonderful endeavor,

whether it is making a donation to a deserving organization or volunteering at a homeless shelter. We are taught that giving is preferable than receiving.

66.
67. But often, we put others' needs ahead of our own. When was the last time you took action just because it made you feel good? How recently have you thought lovingly of yourself? Go ahead; I'll give you some time to consider it. Okay, the allotted time has expired. I firmly think that whatever we do ultimately stems from our desire to feel happy. If you keep giving and giving while feeling angry about it, you will undoubtedly continue to draw situations that will allow you to feel greater resentment. However, you eventually gain from those positive sensations if you are feeling good about whatever it is and you are aware of when you are.

68.
69. I am aware that everything beautiful appears to emerge in my life whenever I am enthused about anything. Many, many years ago, when I was in a

brand-new relationship, I recall how the enthusiasm over that caused other happy events. I was giving metaphysics lectures at the time. Usually, it appeared like I had trouble getting people to sign up for the class. But as soon as I entered that relationship, I enrolled in one of my biggest courses ever. In other words, positive thoughts and sentiments lead to positive outcomes.

70.

71.   My wife and I made the decision to go to Alaska on our maiden cruise a few years ago. About that, we were quite thrilled! Who would not? At the time, we lacked the whole amount needed for the trip. However, we had been giving metaphysical lectures for a while. Students at two of the courses we conducted appeared to arrive out of nowhere. These two sessions were almost entirely filled, and the money they brought in covered the majority of the cost of our trip. That probably wouldn't have occurred if we hadn't been anticipating our cruise.

72.

73.   Once again, the Law of Attraction reacts to the energy you project into the world. And in those two instances, that is precisely what took place. "The better it gets, the better it gets!" is one of my favorite sayings."

74.

75.   And the more you search for good in your life, the more likely it is that good will find you rather than the other way around. We are constantly energetically crossing paths with other people, things, and situations. And whether we are in a good mood, beautiful mood, or joyous mood, life will organize itself such that we cross paths with something that corresponds to those higher emotional states.

76.

77.   So it's advantageous for you to feel good about it. No, you won't always feel terrific. However, the more you practice feeling great, amazing, or joyous, the more you are preparing for meeting your ideal soul partner. Additionally, don't be scared to take care of yourself

so that you can feel wonderful. When you do, life is more enjoyable.

78.

A HALF WOMAN DRAWS A HALF MAN

Doug, Kara's boyfriend, gave her the evil look as she laughed. "I was only having fun. You take things much too seriously," she said as she shoveled more potato chips into her mouth.

Since she had put on five pounds in the previous month, she definitely should have stuck to salad, but she was getting those urges once again and was unable to resist. In addition, if Doug really loved her as much as he said, he shouldn't object if she gains a few pounds, right?

She questioned if he really loved her based on how he was behaving just now. He was exaggerating a little issue. She had just agreed on Facebook with a pal that she would sleep with Jason Kirkwood, the newest twenty-something Hollywood sensation.

She was aware that Doug would read the message, but she had no clue that he would take offense to it. It was as if he were some kind of sacred virgin. She would never believe he had never thought in such sexual terms about famous ladies.

Doug now stared at her as he placed his hamburger on the ground. "Kara, what's wrong with you?"

Kara gulped down the mouthful and scowled. What exactly is wrong with me, do you mean? I'm hardly the most sensitive person around.

You believe I approve of your sleeping with other men?"

Kara was beginning to regret making the post, saying, "Like I'd ever have the chance to really do it." Or she never added Doug as a friend on Facebook.

His gaze was concentrated on her. "What if you ever had the opportunity? You would?"

"Oh my God, I can't believe that - "

Will you?"

Kara's jaw became clenched. "Yes, perhaps I would,"

Doug took her one more look before getting up slowly from the chair. I'm leaving the area.

"Doug? What's your destination? Doug!"

******

This may be an exaggerated example of the concept of this chapter, but you have to confront the reality: if you have had several heartbreaks, it's likely that you aren't yet deserving of your soul mate. You still need to mature a little. That has nothing to do with your age; it has everything to do with discovering what true love is, since love cannot exist in an environment where selfishness, as Kara exemplifies in the case above.

Having stated that, I also need to highlight that life is a process and that no one ever fully realizes their ideal selves while they are on this planet. You will never be able to resolve all of your personal concerns, no matter how hard you try. Not even your soul partner will.

And if you wait until you are perfect before looking for him, you will live a lonely and empty existence.

However, if you want to find — and maintain — the love of your life, you must have attained a certain degree of maturity. What type of person do you think you'll end up with if you're selfish, careless, and unfaithful?

Right. Let's go through the fundamental ways you may start to be ready for your soul mate so that you don't wind up with that sort of person.

Recognize your feminine needs.

This was briefly discussed previously, but I'd want to expand on it now. Women need to be understood, cared for, and devoted by their life partners more than anything else. We want their respect and confidence just as much.

Even if our wants and those of men are partly similar, they are distinct enough that it is beneficial to be aware of them. Why is it important to be conscious of your needs? One reason is that you can interact with your lover more effectively when you are.

Jerry worried a lot about our money during the first four years of our marriage, particularly after the 2008 financial crisis and when his firm started laying off employees in his field. When Jerry became despondent about money, I became concerned and angry as well since one of my greatest anxieties as a single woman was not having enough money to take care of myself. I explicitly told him many times, "You're not making me feel comfortable, and I need it!"

I didn't intend for him to mislead me about his emotions or the health of his finances. Simply put, I wanted him to have greater faith that everything would turn out for the best and that we wouldn't lose everything. He had to have confidence in the face of difficulty for me to feel secure.

Being conscious of your emotional needs will also help you avoid burdening your soul mate too much. He won't always fulfill your wants the way you want him to since he is not more flawless than you are. That's reasonable given that you won't always fulfill his demands in the manner he desires.

You'll do well to keep your expectations in check in this regard, whether you're single or in an exclusive relationship. I, like with many other women, find it beneficial to rely on both God and our companions to keep us grounded and strong. As much as he loves you, your soul partner will undoubtedly have terrible days and challenging times.

Our kid was a huge struggle when he was a toddler. He consumed all of our attention and energy, notably that of Jerry, who almost stopped giving me unplanned non-sexual touches as a result. I would beg him for attention for approximately three days, and then, it seemed to me, he would forget about me once again.

Do not fool yourself into believing that your soul partner would be Mr. Romance and never act inappropriately as mine has; those were difficult times. If you really believe that, allow me to explain why you keep having heartbreak after heartbreak right now.

How did I respond to it, then? Did I deceive him? abused him? No! I approached him, gave him a kiss and a hug, and told him I loved him. I also expressed my desire for him to do more of it with me.

Our youngster eventually calmed down a little, and Jerry had the energy to start attending to my needs once again. Knowing what I needed helped me to maintain objectivity rather than being very frustrated, which may have escalated into real resentment against my spouse. I was able to wait out the storm because to my improved mindset as a result of this viewpoint.

The ability to better understand your attraction to a man is a third reason to be conscious of your requirements. I had a crush on someone who was not meant to be mine in my early thirties. He was paying me more attention than anybody had in a long time, which was the key factor. He had no idea that he was satisfying my desire for loyalty and security.

Although I didn't find him physically beautiful, the fact that he met those two criteria was enough for me to develop a hidden admiration for him. Due to my lack of awareness of my requirements, I ultimately suffered a shattered heart and damaged relationship.

If a guy who is not your soul mate satisfies one or two of your emotional requirements while you wait for "the one" to come along, it is not immoral. But if you don't answer him right, you can suffer a shattered heart or, worse still, commit to a man who turns out to be the wrong one.

Be accountable.

Women often express their dissatisfaction with their partners and spouses' lack of responsibility. Guess what, though? One of the main complaints that guys have about women is also this one. A half-woman will draw a half-man. You must learn to be responsible with all of those things if you want a guy who is responsible with his money, time, resources, abilities, etc.

Given that one of the main sources of marital strife is money, it may be better to use this as an example. I'm going to have to be firm for a second: if you buy for clothing and other items every weekend that you don't need, you are not being financially responsible. Additionally, you are moving down broken-heart alley.

To care for their wife, males put in endless hours of labour. How do you think it affects them to be unable to invest or preserve any of it because their wife can't pass up that adorable clothing, which they will most likely never wear? How content do you think your partner would be if you make him work longer hours to satisfy your materialistic needs? How would you feel knowing that you'll never get to spend time with him because you can't wait to have what you want?

Yes, I am aware that guys borrow money to pay for toys like boats, four-wheelers, and other items. I am aware that many males are as careless with money. But what's this? You're making an effort not to entice one of those men! You want someone who can budget his spending and put money down for retirement. You must thus live within your means and have spare money to save.

Since I started working at age 16, I have always been very frugal with my money. Who did I draw in? A guy who, on an average wage, had the funds to, among other things, purchase me an absurdly expensive engagement ring, take me on our honeymoon to Maui, pay off our mortgage within five years of purchasing our home, and still retire early!

Yes, it really does pay off! - to improve yourself while you wait for your true love to show up. As a result, practice being accountable in all aspects of your life, not just financial ones.

Be compassionate.

Question of the day: Was Kara being kind in the opening scene of this chapter? You get an A++ if you responded "No!"

If there is one thing that my years of marriage to Jerry have taught me, it is that men like being taken care of. particularly when they are ill. When they're sick, our strong, bulky guys who can defeat lions moan the loudest. This is the reason why it's often remarked that it's a good thing that males don't have to be the ones who have children. Women just tend to be better able to deal with illness and discomfort in general than males.

But your boyfriend will want you to show concern in situations other than illness. Do you still recall his crippling concern about feeling fake? His desire for confidence and approval? He needs to know that you care by being the largest supporter of him and by telling and demonstrating your confidence in him.

However, I must issue you with one warning in this regard. Men do not want to speak out their difficulties as women do. When you bombard a man with inquiries when he is plainly sad or depressed, it doesn't make him feel cared for; rather, it makes him feel badgered, nagged, and distrusted!

He doesn't want to discuss his issues; instead, he wants some privacy so he can come up with a solution on his own. You may use a phrase like "Bad day, huh?But when you ask incisive questions, you give him the impression that you don't trust him to handle his own difficulties, so it's better to say, "Let me know if I can do anything" or, "Let me know if I can do anything." And being able to do so is a significant factor in a man feeling worthwhile and appreciated.

You might also indicate your concern by:

be dependable,

be devoted,

be curious about his life,

(The saying "the way to a man's heart is through his stomach" is true, sweetheart!) Prepare his favorite dish, and

Whenever he is working on hobbies or projects, hang out with him.

How does a single individual go about doing that?

Talk less and listen more to your friends and family members.

Asking about other people's life demonstrates your interest in them.

Where you notice a need, provide assistance, money, or a meal.

Be courteous while using social media.

Make contact with a buddy you haven't spoken to in a long.

You may need to master the delicate balance between being the typical doormat and demonstrating that you care if you are sanguine or phlegmatic. In order to say "no" and to end harmful relationships, you must also take care of yourself.

However, if you have a history of several failed relationships, there's a strong likelihood that your capacity for compassion may need some improvement. Your selfish actions are either repelling nice men or luring in the wrong crowd. So start working on being a better lover, honey!

Don't be a parasite.

Men like feeling needed. They like feeling helpful. They really like helping out their spouse.

Time for a harsh reality: guys are not drawn to women who behave as if they can handle everything on their own. Buy a ticket out of it if you've bought into the feminist mantra that you need to be independent. If you are sincere about finding your One and Only, that is.

Yes, I am aware that being single requires you to be resourceful. I've already done that. But learning to let go of certain things and ask for assistance is a necessary step in becoming the woman who can draw the guy you desire.

Getting back to the subject of the title, males don't like leeches yet preferring to be needed. They dislike women who are too dependent, whiny, or clinging. The fundamental cause is that, in contrast to women, males are not naturally nurturing. People who require continuous attention drain them of all their energy, which leaves them disappointed, dejected, and sometimes even furious.

He doesn't want to spend the whole time listening to you rant about your emotions while you hang out with your partner. He doesn't want to learn that you can't use a vacuum after you are married or that you can't boil water! He doesn't want you to mourn over his departure or nag him about doing it if he's the kind to dash off to the north woods and go fishing with friends for a few weeks every year.

Men appreciate women who require assistance with heavy lifting, construction projects, or toilet repairs. Leeches, on the other hand, are ladies who are persistently unfavorable or inept.

Get control of your feelings.

This idea is strongly related to the last one since, if you can master your emotions, you won't be a leech.

What does "get in control" mean? Does it imply that you should repress your emotions and never weep again? Nevermind that idea! Just ask Jerry; I cry a lot! It promotes mental and physical wellness, which may be why women often live longer than males.

But you must keep in mind that you and your soul mate have distinct wiring. Your girlfriends don't mind if you weep for hours on end on their shoulders. Even better, they converse with you back and tell their own relevant tales. They adore such things and could do it all day long, just like you.

Men? Not really. In fact, many people find it impossible to do that kind of activity for more than two minutes without experiencing throat tightening and head spinning. A member of them is Jerry. Even though I'm not angry with him, he shuts down and withdraws when I truly let my emotions run wild. He just isn't capable of handling too much emotion at once.

Other men who are unable to manage it get enraged and begin shouting. Which won't aid in your gaining composure.

So, here are some pointers to help you start learning how to regain control of yourself.

Keep the majority of your response to anything to yourself and your bedroom mirror. Be more subdued in public.

Even better, develop the practice of adopting many viewpoints. You won't respond the same way as you would if you assumed that the woman who cut you off in traffic had just received a call informing her that one of her children had been seriously injured.

Prior to speaking, practice controlling your emotions. Take deep breaths while gently counting to 10. Twenty times, squish a soft ball in your hand as hard as you can. Do something subtly that will allow you to calm yourself before speaking would help.

Do you need to make a decision between life and death? Since we women have a talent for making molehills into mountains, let's face it, girlfriend.

One or more of the following may lessen the intensity of your P.M.S. mood swings, if not completely eradicate them, if they have resulted in at least one breakup for you:

Keep an eye on your cycle and get familiar with your mood/behavior patterns. Being aware of when you are going to have a difficult time might help you get over it more quickly (for example, saying, "I'm so depressed, but I know I'll get over it tomorrow because my period starts next week" is preferable to saying, "Why am I always so depressed? I might as well just give up on life.").

Become less stressed overall.

Change your diet from processed to whole foods.

Avoid gluten.

Start taking chelated magnesium supplements; they will be quite helpful if you have restless legs.

As soon as your emotions start to spin out of control, use therapeutic-grade lavender, rosemary, and/or geranium essential oil. (Search for oils from brands with higher ethical standards than others, such as Native American Nutritionals, Butterfly Express, or Be Young Essential Oils.)

Be mindful of your health.

Feed your body foods that you are certain are healthy, and save occasional indulgences in junk food. three to four times every week, go for a walk. Consider reading more instead of watching TV or browsing the web.

Master stress management. Become in touch with God. Take a multivitamin with a whole-foods basis; two of the finest brands are Garden of Life's "Vitamin Code" and New Chapter.

Avoid being anorexic (if you are anorexic, read the following section) or becoming preoccupied with dieting. However, do not neglect your personal hygiene. It's about having more energy, sharper focus and mood, glowing skin, not about not being overweight (or attempting to be tiny). Being conscious of your health—and responsible for maintaining it—will enhance your attractiveness and draw men who are conscientious about their own health.

Why is that relevant? You'll both continue to be desirable to one another, and you'll both be less likely to get one of those terrible illnesses that take too many lives too soon. In other words, happy soul mates have more time together on this planet.

HOW TO FIND YOUR LIFE'S PERFECT PARTNER

Do you want to find real love? Do you daydream about the guy of your dreams? Do you want to master the art of attraction in order to draw your ideal spouse to you? Well, this post might provide you with some helpful advice and pointers for wooing a guy.

Finding a suitable companion might be a challenging challenge, but getting him to fall for you could be much harder. It is very upsetting to see other attractive women swarming your lovely man. You must thus learn some enticing advice, like the following:

Be Mysterious - Men like mysteries, and they enjoy solving them even more. Don't provide all of your personal information at the first encounter. Leave certain things unsaid and give in to his insatiable curiosity. Be distant and covert.

Men like ladies who are clean and have a pleasant floral scent. Make sure to have your hair done and to get your nails done. Possess a positive mindset and a fantastic personality. That way, you've already won half the fight.

Be Confident and use your confidence to entice a guy. Men prefer assertive women who demand respect. But avoid being arrogant and overconfident. He may get defensive or become scared as a result. Inform him about your admirable goals and future objectives. Men value women who are driven to succeed in their life.

Be at ease and genuine; don't attempt to fake it in order to attract the real guy. One of the biggest turnoffs, maybe. Simply strive to be your true, admirable self and let people see you for who you really are.

Be Realistic – Stop seeking for the ideal partner that fulfills all of your expectations. Make some sensible concessions. Be realistic and don't expect your partner to beg for your hand while on his knees; he could be too timid to do such filmy things. Nevertheless, avoid frightening or embarrassing your guy by going above and above to win his favor.

However, it's also crucial that you get the correct type of attention from decent guys rather than lecherous Romeos who are trying to take advantage of you. Some guys just want to have fun and get excited at your cost. Most males still see women as just objects of desire. You are going to walk on thin glass in your hunt for the ideal mate, so proceed with caution.

After all the fun and games, some poor ladies are left high and dry by dishonest guys. Avoid being involved with these incorrect guys. They can only be painful and hurtful. Find that ideal partner that seems straightforward but really has a golden heart. The strength of this man's love can fulfill all of your desires.

However, if you end up falling for the wrong man, don't get disheartened and begin to believe that there are no more nice guys on earth. There are still good, moral guys out there yearning for their ladylove. Choose one and make him feel drawn to you like a magnet.

At some time in our lives, everyone looks for a life mate. We all want them to be just as good as gold. But do we really know what we want from a relationship? What qualities are we looking for in a partner?

Let's be really honest with ourselves. Do we possess the qualities necessary to entice the ideal mate into our lives? The majority of us lack an answer. We frequently get perplexed and begin to delve deeply into our awareness. Some believe they have it inside them, but words alone cannot convince. Words never speak as loudly as actions.

Try to identify all the idealistic characteristics that you are seeking in a soul partner. The following may be useful.

My ideal mate should be very nice, giving, and wealthy. He should also be devoted, dependable, and caring. Most importantly, he should accept me for who I am and be prepared for a healthy long-term relationship. He ought to accept me for who I am, flaws and all.

Many of us struggle with self-confidence and worry that we won't be able to meet the demands of our future spouse. To attract and be attracted, such ideas need to be banished. We ought to be self-assured and confident. In contrast to others, we shouldn't feel poor or inferior. The only way the other person will love and respect you is if you first love and respect yourself.

Let's look at some tips for finding the ideal partner: o Be extroverted and pleasant with others. Always smile instead of making a lengthy, irritated face. o Surround yourself with kind and caring individuals because their energy will spread to you. o Take care of oneself; engage in artistic pursuits like writing, reading, candlemaking, etc. o Always presentable with nice appearance and tidy demeanor. o Don't have expectations for people; 99% of the time, they will let you down. o Be kind to everyone; do not carry any ill will or malice for anybody. These unfavorable feelings will reduce your attractiveness. o Be resolute and committed. Be assertive when necessary and approach life with confidence in general.

These things are easier said than done, but with a little effort and self-reflection, you can correct your dumb errors and yourself. For example, if you are angry and resentful with someone, they may feel the same way about you. And if you don't manage your thoughts and behaviors, these negative emotions can start to spread and you might start to become even more pessimistic. It is preferable to banish these negative ideas from our minds and replace them with positive, enjoyable ones.

The change will come slowly and gradually, but you'll notice that people are more drawn to you than they were before, and they all have good intentions. Everyone wants a decent, loving person in their life.

God only gives us what we deserve, not what we desire, according to the universal truth. If you are kind, good, loving, and loyal, you will discover a spouse who has the same wonderful traits.

God will provide you with a wonderful life partner if you can find perfection inside your spirit.

The Real Definition of The Ideal Partner

With the possible exception of the person who is your biggest support, there is no clear description of the ideal mate. We all want for the Mr. or Mrs. Right who will prove to be the ideal life partner. Spending your whole life alone is difficult. We all need someone to love us, take care of us, and be there for us while we're struggling as people. When both partners complement one another and hide one other's flaws, a relationship is ideal.

It is true that every successful guy has a lady at his side. But it's also true that every successful woman has a guy at her side. This adage is accurate when referring to a perfect union. Someone who will comprehend your goals and support and assist you in achieving them is the ideal spouse. He or she is your best friend, supporter, and critic. A great spouse would play the cards sensibly for a long and fulfilling relationship because they would know you inside and out.

You'll never experience relationship stress if your companion is ideal. There are very little possibilities of misinterpretation or misunderstandings since your spouse fully understands you. He or she is someone who has whole faith in you and provides you the personal space you need. There is a great deal of mutual respect among the participants, as well as the appropriate degree of independence. When you can trust your spouse, you naturally give them space to act independently when necessary, which in turn makes the connection stronger.

A person who accepts you as you are and doesn't attempt to alter you is the ideal companion. Your better half will always treat you with respect, no matter what you signify to the world. Deals and a wish list of materialistic requirements have no place in a genuine relationship. Your better half is someone who gives you encouragement when you feel like the world is against you. He or she is someone who supports you no matter what.

A wonderful partner is someone who serves as a lover, friend, teacher, and guardian when necessary. At every stage of life, they energize the partnership and perform a variety of functions. When your love for each other is equal and compatible, and when your wavelengths align, you are in a great relationship. Both parties must be prepared to put in the work to create the ideal connection; only then can they really be described as soul mates.

When you discover the right life mate, a relationship seems to be a gift because of the degree of understanding and unending love. Finding the right companion takes more than just chance; but, if you think about a few things before making a commitment, you are likely to meet your ideal match. Make sure you have some similar interests, preferences, and dislikes before choosing somebody. Spending time together allows you to really understand one another before becoming closer. Join dating websites or start attending events that are well-known. Finding your ideal mate and meeting some intriguing individuals will both be much easier by doing this.

The Top Mistakes to Avoid When Seeking Your Ideal Partner

Finding the right spouse or real love is a difficult but not impossible undertaking. A lot of people who had the appropriate mindset and approach discovered true love. However, there are several traps that you must dodge in order to go in for the kill!

When looking for your ideal spouse, the following are some of the top errors to avoid:

Being impatient - You need to have a lot of patience for wonderful things to occur. Being impatient won't do while you're looking for your ideal partner. Your boyfriend may also experience that you are eager to have him join your group. He could flee from you as a result of it. Therefore, exercise patience and provide your potential mate some breathing room. You are not on a racecourse, so there is no need to gallop faster, for you may actually lose the match rather than win it.

Conversing Powers - When your partner speaks to you, do not keep on about your daily schedules or activities. Your partner needs to know the real you, not what you are doing 24 x 7. Just try to let him get a glimpse of your character and the kind of person you really are. Don't bore him about your dog's antics or how adorable your kid sister is.

Being Tense - If you are not relaxed and comfortable, you tend to make the other person also equally uncomfortable. And no one likes to be in the company of people who make them squirm and ill at ease. The main thing is to be relaxed, and that can add a special glow to your face also.

Mr. Superman - Most of us looking for the perfect soul mate feel that the moment one arrives in our life they would take over all our problems or that troubles may mysteriously disappear. Well, you can't be more wrong. What do you think? Is he is some kind of magical helper or Mr. Fix all? He can be a good helping hand, and that's all to it. Do not expect him to perform magic-he is no God. It would be really ironical if your partner expected the same kind of magic help from you too.

Being Impractical - Sometimes, when you are so intensely searching for your Mr. Right, you fail to see that there are many suitable men near you. And you may actually let go that very person whom you are seeking, from right under your nose. So the key is to be practical and grounded, don't literally live in a dreamland. Keep your eyes and ears open.

You often draw into your life those individuals that are similar to you. They behave and have personalities like you do. People who are similar to you will be drawn to you, according to the law of attraction. If you are impatient and desperate, you could find a mate who is also impatient and desperate.

Therefore, the secret is to reinvent yourself, look inside, and become better every day.

And you'll be shocked to discover that one day all your mistakes and challenges finding your ideal relationship are magically erased, and your ideal lover is waiting for you with open arms.

The Myths Preventing Us From Finding The Ideal Partner

Why do we need to follow rigid rules in order to find our ideal companions when love is a lovely sensation that is open and spontaneous?

Several false beliefs that prevent us from meeting our ideal companion include:

Working hard to establish a wonderful relationship is not necessary if you and your spouse are connected by a strong sense of love and trust. Work is not needed to support love; rather, a compromise of some type is needed. If you often argue and experience discord, you may have picked the incorrect spouse. Maintain the love quotient while making sacrifices: Compromises and sacrifices are like attempting to glue together a vase's shattered parts. Frequent requests for sacrifice, particularly when they are made only for the benefit of the other spouse, is a telltale indicator that the relationship is steadily deteriorating. Healthy sacrifices from both parties are necessary for true love. attempting to alter the partner's behavior: Change need to originate within. Have you heard the adage, "Our flaws and improper behavior aggravate us most when we see it in others"? There must be something wrong with us if we are unhappy with the kind of person we appear to attract. Before evaluating others, we must first make changes to ourselves. In the dream, you can be looking for a relationship or perhaps your soul match. It is just a fantasy for someone to save you from the evil guys or a flat tire. You need to get up because it may never happen. In the event of a flat tire, a decent woman or an elderly uncle may take the place of the attractive hunk. Be sensible and grounded. The more you immerse yourself in imagination, the more it will influence your mundane and uninteresting actual reality. They continued to live blissfully till the very end of their lives. This is undoubtedly fiction; no pair could maintain a continual state of happiness. Periodic arguments, upsets, and reconciliations are necessary for a healthy relationship since they contribute to the true flavor of life. Think about how monotonous it would be if the couple was constantly happy and in love with one another. Happy ever after ought to signify something different than what you may expect from a fairy tale. Your need for a specific someone to really make you happy Being happy is an internal experience; you decide whether to be happy or miserable. If you don't like who you are, no one else can change that, I promise you that. He or she could temporarily ease your hurting heart, but after a while, everything will return to its original gloomy state. Try to be content and pleased with yourself; the world may have its turn at some point.

Life is a mirror; it reflects our image of ourselves, not what we wish to see. It's necessary to respect, treat oneself with dignity, and act with love and assurance. And you'll be shocked to learn that everyone else is treating you well.

Largest Myths Regarding Finding Your Ideal Partner Online

The majority of American singles are members of well-known online dating services where they search for their ideal partner. There are examples of dating that have been successful.

Sites are a terrific method to browse profiles and discover the ideal spouse. Numerous dating websites exist to assist individuals in meeting others who share their preferences, hobbies, and worldviews. You may pick a person to meet by reading their profile and chatting with them to learn more about them before you decide to meet. By doing this, you avoid getting the erroneous date.

Hundreds of individuals have found love thanks to dating websites, however there are several major misunderstandings surrounding meeting your ideal spouse online. Many individuals have the belief that finding love on dating websites is just not feasible. The reality is that you may most definitely use the Internet to meet your ideal soul mate. It is undoubtedly different from the conventional methods of meeting people at work or college, but it does aid in your search for the ideal match. The huge number of unions between people who met internet speaks for itself. There is a significant probability that you will find your future spouse online.

Another dating site fallacy I've run through is that they're unsafe. It's true that there haven't been many reports of ladies being tricked and deceived on dating websites, but did any of them know they had signed up for fake sites? Don't just register on any website you choose at random. Before signing up as a member, you must confirm the legitimacy and security of the website. All reputable and professional dating sites have security measures in place and demand that users act in a certain way in order to protect themselves.

Another myth about meeting the right companion online is that only attractive profiles or people in prominent positions in their professions do so. This isn't really the case. I agree that in order to attract attention, one must make an attractive profile and submit a lovely photo, but that does not imply that others have no possibility of finding love. After all, a person choose to date based on their compatibility and shared interests. Regarding occupation, the websites are populated by individuals from many walks of life. You will discover folks from every imaginable profession, including physicians, engineers, students, and truck drivers. Simply look for someone who fits your requirements.

Many newcomers think using dating services is a difficult procedure. This could be something to consider before you start, but it won't make sense afterwards. You would be astonished to learn how simple it is to browse these sites if you pick the correct dating site. To manage the website, you don't need to be an expert in computers.

It's time you opened your eyes to the facts if you have been preventing yourself from signing up on dating websites just because you believe these falsehoods. For sincere individuals looking for love and a suitable spouse, dating websites are ideal. You can make an informed choice about who to date by getting to know a select group of individuals.

ARE YOU PREPARED FOR A SEVERE HIP-HOP DIET?

"And they feel their hearts are at home when they finally have the opportunity to meet. Where they belong, at home. The basis of their connection and friendship allows them to forge an unbreakable relationship. All they can do all day is enjoy one other's company." - Unknown

A Serious Relationship: What Is It?

Signs You're All Set

Flings aren't meant to last a lifetime and might be stressful. So how about tracking down the real deal? Are you unsure about whether you should start looking for anything significant at this point in your life? Examine the points below first, then.

A Serious Relationship: What Is It?

It's important to comprehend what this kind of connection with someone else entails in order to determine if you're really at the point in your life where you're ready to be in a committed relationship. In its purest form, a serious relationship is one in which both partners are fully committed to one another, are forthright and honest with one another, have complete faith in one another, and share the same values and goals for the future.

There isn't a certain age, achievement, or turning point that may indicate when you should be in a committed relationship, but you should go within and be honest with yourself about what you actually want and feel right now.

What to Look for in a Serious Relationship

There are five key indications to look out for if you're attempting to decide whether to go on a journey in search of "the one" in order to determine whether or not a serious relationship is the best choice for you at this time.

You want to devote your whole life to someone else.

Whether you're unsure of your readiness for a committed relationship, you should be thrilled by the prospect of giving someone else your undivided attention. In other words, a committed relationship could be a satisfying option for you if you're looking for both emotional and physical connection. You're not yet ready to be in a serious relationship, however, if you're more interested in dating other people and having loose connections.

You Are Aware of Your Partner's Qualities

When you're prepared for a committed relationship, you should be aware of the traits and characteristics you want in a partner. You should specifically decide what qualities you seek in a potential partner. Is it vital for your partner to share your political views, yoga passion, or even your religion, for instance? Once you are aware of what you value in another person, you can begin to build the foundation for a relationship based on mutual worth in all areas.

Make sure what you're asking for is realistic while thinking about the qualities you want in a partner. This will ensure that your expectations are reasonable and prevent you from being disappointed in the future after the honeymoon period.

You've had your fill of excuses.

Because they believe they lack the time or energy that a genuine connection requires, people often shy away from engaging in such relationships. For instance, many people with demanding work schedules refrain from looking for serious relationships because they believe they can't give the other person the proper amount of attention. But if you're really prepared for a committed relationship, you'll stop making up excuses for not pursuing your goals. In fact, you'll be able to prioritize and prepare so that your obligations at work and elsewhere don't prevent you from forming deep connections with other people.

Examine what you are really preventing yourself from if you find yourself making excuses all the time. Ask yourself honestly: Are you really too busy at work, or are there underlying concerns about romantic commitment that you need to address?

You don't feel any pressure to date seriously

When you are really prepared for a committed relationship, it is because you want one. In truth, you must make this kind of life-altering decision by yourself. And if your partner, your family, or your friends are pressuring you to enter into this kind of serious commitment before you're ready or interested in doing so, you're setting yourself up for failure later on.

You Have a Risk-Taking Attitude

Finally, it's critical to understand that looking for a meaningful connection necessitates taking a risk. In particular, you are not only making yourself emotionally exposed and wholly available to someone else, but you are also risking your heart. You won't be able to enjoy the closeness that a meaningful relationship may bring, however, since a part of you is still jealously guarded, if you don't take this major step of trust. The good news is that you'll be able to take this kind of risk and have the fulfilling relationship that you deserve when you're actually ready to explore a deeper connection with someone else.

THE REAL STORY OF ONLINE DATING

Online dating is still seen by some as taboo, something you don't really discuss with your friends. If you do happen to meet someone online, you'll merely make up a narrative to share with them. However, internet dating has gained popularity in the dating world, and the fact is that many of women use this platform to locate a spouse. Knowing that many women are now using the internet to locate their soul mate is not unexpected. Utilizing this approach offers advantages, including the fact that it is less uncomfortable and doesn't demand you to leave the house. What is it like to date online, then? Is this the only answer to finding the ideal companion in the current world? Or is this simply another means through which women might learn about the negative aspects and hells of dating? Before we discuss any of those dating success ideas, it's important to keep in mind that, like every dating strategy, online dating has its benefits and drawbacks.

Pros

You can be certain that everyone you meet via internet dating is single. There are several options, so you don't have to keep checking clubs and hoping to find someone who is sufficiently appealing. With online dating, you may pick from thousands of guys with various origins, looks, occupations, ages, and hobbies. All it takes is one click to express interest.

In online dating, you are also in command of everything. You'll wind up reducing your expectations merely to hunt for someone if you've tried hanging out in pubs where there are about a hundred men (not all of them are genuinely single or may not even like you). If you look online, this is not the case. Here, you may get requests from hundreds of men, and you may choose to ignore the majority of them, respond to some of them, or think about going out with a limited number of them.

Before going on a date, you may also politely and without being like a griller ask the man questions. You may enquire about their preferences in anything from fundamental political beliefs and principles to music, movies, and hobbies. If things don't work out in the end, it is also simple to reject a candidate without having to deal with conflict with the buddy who set you up on the date. You may look at your second option after you have eliminated a person from your possible list since they will just fade into obscurity in the online dating arena.

Online multi-dating is another option. In actuality, avoiding many dates is difficult. There's no use in being fixated on just one person as you'll still be talking to, looking at, or messaging other possible dates even if you won't be seeing two people at once. Since someone else will inform you that he is in a message format, you are less likely to instantly fall in love with someone in this situation or stress out if you discover that he isn't truly into you.

Cons

You're not truly seeing the person you're dating, which is a given. They simply provide a single picture on their profile, and it is up to you to determine if you like the person or not. Most of the time, photos may be deceptive. In addition to how individuals seem in photos—which are often better than they are in person—good lighting, angles, and shadows also have an impact—you can't tell anything about someone's height, build, or whether or not they have really small hands from just one image. You should thus remember to stay away from profiles with little images. There are almost no assurances, but the more images that are accessible, the better.

The chemistry between you and your possible date is another thing to think about. Being completely OK in an email is not the same as being completely fine in person. Yes, your date may be an Adonis, and you may have enjoyed exchanging great emails for some time, but when you actually see him in person, there is just nothing, leaving you to wonder how you can survive the evening with this guy.

Additionally, online dating will make you very picky. Initially, your criteria could be quite straightforward, but as time goes on, they'll become more difficult to meet. It is difficult to overcome the fact that you will eventually have no one good enough for you.

Additionally, you face opposition. Online, you face up against ladies from diverse backgrounds and corners of the globe. You could be one of a few, if not the only, beautiful ladies in the bar. However, hundreds of gorgeous women are flirting and presenting their wares online, including their appealing traits and skills. Be aware that there are more attractive women than males online. And certainly, that may be inconvenient.

Additionally time-consuming is online dating. It may rule your life! You'll get messages from guys who like you, and you'll need to like them back. Just before your date with another man, one of the guys offers you his phone number, and the other calls you for a talk. In addition, you still need to consider your job, friends, and general way of life. Your brain may want to burst at this point.

Not all men you meet online are seeking for a relationship. It's not always true that someone is seeking for a serious relationship just because they are looking for dates. Some of the males you'll encounter are just dating their way out of a prior relationship because they haven't moved beyond it. Some people have been through so much suffering that they need to injure a few women to get through it. Others just don't want anything committed and see internet dating as a convenient method to hook up. Therefore, before moving forward with a prospective date, find out as soon as you can about their prior relationships. This will assist you in avoiding unpleasant shocks.

Online dating has its ups and downs, just like any other way of meeting possible companions. Before you acquire advice on how to successfully discover the right guy, it's crucial to understand both sides of the industry!

USING DATING WEBSITES ONLINE

It's time to go out and acquire what you want since you're quite confident you know what you want. People struggle because the adage "good things come to those who wait" isn't really accurate or beneficial in this situation or in other areas of life. The sheer number of individuals I've met (particularly women) who lazily wonder why they're single is difficult to put into words. I don't believe that women are to blame for this; we have been socialized to believe that males should initiate contact. Although this may be immensely romantic, there are times when it just isn't the case. The truth is that just desiring and earning a decent companion is insufficient. Regardless of your gender identity or sexual orientation, you must be proactive in your hunt for "the one."

Do not confuse being proactive with trying to date as many guys (or women) as you can. The list in Chapter Two ought to have some use. If you can avoid it, don't waste your time or theirs beyond the first date or even before the first date if a possible date isn't what you're looking for in any of the areas that are essential to you.

Using a dating site is one of the simplest methods to focus on a certain sort of person. Use of dating websites to find a long-term spouse or simply new friendships has grown widespread among those between the ages of twenty and thirty. When your friends learn you have a dating profile, you could feel a little more shame if you're older. Do not let stigma weigh you down because of your age. Dating services are just tools that use the internet's now-ubiquitous technology to assist you in finding love. It's no stranger—in fact, it's a lot more practical—than meeting someone at a bar or a friend's party. If you and the individual whose profile you are looking at answered the questionnaires honestly, you have a higher chance of finding a compatible partner on a dating website than you do at any of the aforementioned social gatherings.

In some respects, the internet may be a terrific litmus test to screen out the poor ones before meeting in person, even while it is true that you should meet someone in person to evaluate compatibility. In contrast, if the chat is clunky and uncomfortable, the individual is probably not worth pursuing. If you can already conduct a terrific conversation online. The one situation in which you may want to reject this piece of advice is if the individual confesses to texting poorly yet comes off as interesting enough for you to want to learn more. Perhaps offer a Skype or phone conversation in this situation.

It might be a little daunting to pick from the various dating websites available. However, you can quickly determine which is the best to establish an account on based on your age range, sexual preference, and intended use. It would be better to avoid using apps like Tinder or Grindr as this book is about finding a soul partner. Admittedly, on apps like these, a decent connection may sometimes be established. However, these websites were primarily developed as a quick method to locate a hookup. There is almost any room to write about yourself on Tinder, and users only express their feelings by swiping left or right. This is the online version of meeting a hot stranger in a bar.

More beneficial programs and websites include the very well-liked Match, Chemistry, OKCupid (OKC), Plenty of Fish (POF), or eHarmony. When compared to a normal dating site search, they feature a lot more thorough questionnaire system and more precise match screening. These websites are free to use, but upgraded members have privileges such as being shown first in matches and being able to know if someone has read their messages.

On any website, it's crucial (and enjoyable) to complete the questionnaires and profiles completely since that way you have the highest possibility of finding precise matches. Of course, you cannot be sure that everyone else has answered theirs truthfully, but at least you are certain that you haven't hampered yourself. However, being honest does not need total openness. Never give away your address or phone number, or any other personally identifying or sensitive information, while interacting online. Similarly to conventional dating, don't divulge all of your personal information; it's exciting to learn new things about your partner.

Each site has advantages and disadvantages, but they may all appeal to a broad age range and variety of purposes, even if some have developed a reputation for primarily drawing a certain audience in terms of age and purpose. The following are some factors you can find helpful when choosing an appropriate dating site based on the five sites described above.

POF vs. OKC

I would hazard a guess that OKC, for instance, attracts more to folks with strong political beliefs. POF, in contrast, bases its tests on personality-based questions and attraction levels and provides you with "Chemistry Matches," or people who agree with the findings of that chemistry test, in addition to general matches. The "Needs Assessment," "Psychological Assessment," "Keeper Test," and "Sex

Test" are additional tests on POF that assess a range of relationship demands you may have as well as some potential development areas. You may answer any time hundreds of personality quizzes in OKC. Both POF and OKC include Quick Match options, which work something like Tinder's swiping-based matching system but more quickly. On OKC, you may use a match % to direct your swipe decisions. They also provide a quiz that appears periodically and helps you narrow down your matches. It simply takes a little while. The POF rapid match feature lets you focus on the physically you are drawn to. For people who identify as bisexual, OKC is especially helpful since you can modify your filter. You may declare your bisexuality on POF, but you can only match with men or women.

Chemical vs. Physical

You begin Chemistry with its well-known "Personality Quiz," which assigns you to one of four personality types: a Builder, Director, Explorer, or Negotiator. You are questioned on a wide range of topics to find out this, including your finger length, what it looks like when you draw, how many risks you take, and your level of respect for authority. They even inquire as to how you read nonverbal cues. After being asked what qualities (such as religion, smoking habits, physical attractiveness, etc.) you are looking for in a companion, you may begin creating your profile. Your personality type and preferences are taken into consideration when matching you to the ideal personality type for you.

Despite the fact that Chemistry is a subsidiary of Match, I thought Match was far less specific and more suited to the demands someone would have when seeking for a true soul partner. It typically asks the same questions as the aforementioned services, both about you and your prospective partner. The "deal breaker" option is a feature I truly like even if it doesn't go as in-depth as the other sites listed. Referring to the preferences list you created for Chapter Two, it is useful to choose if a possible match's response to each question is a deal breaker.

eHarmony

A renowned dating service, eHarmony is often regarded as the place to seek for your soul partner. Even while you may find this to be the case, it is also renowned as a website for those in their late 30s to middle age. If that describes you, great! If not, feel free to give it a try even if you could discover that you prefer one of the sites suggested above. Additionally, eHarmony offers a sibling website for the LGBTQ community called Compatible Partners. The basic question and scoring methodology used by both websites is the same. You are given a question, and your responses are rated on a scale from "not at all" to "very well" After choosing a few adjectives to use to characterize oneself, the method for rating emotions and way of life returns. Overall, it seems to be a fairly accurate personality test.

Extra Sites

Although I actually would advise using a more well-known website (because more people are probably on them), there are a few specialized websites that are worth mentioning. These include senior-focused websites like Our Time, Farmers Only, and Christian Mingle. It's crucial to go through all the question and answer sections of the website you chose before completing your own profile.

The fact is that soul mates cannot be lost and found. Your soul mate is not lost, thus you don't need to search for them. Your true love is waiting for you. Whether you are prepared for your soul mate is the true question.

It's common for individuals to struggle with practicing self-love on a daily basis, and it's natural to want someone to accept you exactly as you are. However, it might be challenging to love someone else and attract the healthy love you want if you don't love yourself as you are.

It's possible that you're codependent or seeking self-validation if you wish to locate and love your soul mate unreservedly without first loving yourself. If you think you could be codependent or seeking self-validation, this is a problem that has to be addressed and handled.

The risk with these unhealthy dynamics is that you could look to your relationship or your soul match for fulfillment. Consider the situation you would be in if you ever saw the end of that relationship if your sense of self-worth is based on your soul mate, how they make you feel, or your connection. Self-validation must originate from inside, from the conviction that you are deserving of love and that you accept yourself as you are.

Codependency may result from a need for self-validation. Because of their codependent tendencies, individuals may continue in bad relationships because they feel needed or are assured they are loved. As long as they are doing a service, they feel liked or wanted. If you have experienced this or are now doing so, remember that you are more valuable than the services or things you perform for other people.

People can believe they are dependent on you alone for care, and you might agree with them. You must also take care of yourself, however! Despite what you may believe, look back to or read again the traits you listed as desirable in a soul partner. The alternative is that, if you are willing to be misled by fool's gold, you may choose to forego your ideal traits in a soul partner.

Humility has often been used as a justification by those who assert that they can love another person but cannot love themselves. That's one perspective on the matter. But being modest and prioritizing the needs of others are not the only aspects of humility. The capacity to see things clearly is another way to define humility. Try to picture the notion of humility as not being superior to or inferior to another person. This connects to self-love in that you are able to love yourself more completely when you are aware that you are neither more than nor less than another person. Making a list of your flaws takes less time for you. By doing this, you have more time to focus on what you are doing well and how you may better your life and yourself.

One thing to think about is how you can tell when someone is mistreating you if you don't show them affection. The opposite is also accurate. How would you know when you are mistreating people if you don't offer yourself love? Love is an action word, and perfecting anything takes time. You deserve to be loved. When you have self-love, you may effortlessly and guilt-free experience the type of love you desire to attract.

RELATIONSHIPS TO UNDERSTAND

In relationships, nothing is ever straightforward. Men and women are very different beings, let's face it. We vary in the way we see the world, how we respond to various circumstances, and how we interact to one another. Do not feel terrible if you are experiencing relationship difficulties. You can tell that it is not only you if you look around. It is commonplace.

When communication breaks down, relationships often become unhappy. Men and women often say one thing, but mean another. Women may infer the thoughts of other women from what they say, while males can see things differently. Many relationships fail due of this.

You should seek expert counsel if your marriage or partnership seems to be in peril or if you are genuinely struggling in your connection. There are individuals who are more knowledgeable about the distinctions between the sexes and who are equipped to assist you in mending your connections so that they are complete and useful.

Your relationships with your partner will likely be the most difficult ones in your life. While it's true that men will say the same thing about women, the majority of women believe that males are difficult to comprehend. It is true that men and women just have distinct thought processes and speak less. This may cause misconceptions and miscommunications in anyone's interactions.

No matter how much relationship advice one receives, it's challenging to do it properly. Good communication is unquestionably advantageous. But no matter how many words you utter, if you don't comprehend what you're saying, you won't go anywhere. Trying to read more into someone's words than is really there is a typical error that most individuals do in relationships. On the other hand, individuals often fail to pay attention to what their spouse is saying. It only means that things are left unsaid and things are imagined that aren't there. This doesn't mean that either side is right.

There are many sites where you may obtain relationship advice, but keep in mind that some of it may be biased. For people who appear to believe they are poor daters, there are services that are allegedly helpful as well as coaching services. There is no quick fix, although you can discover that you unintentionally convey the incorrect signals. Relationships are mostly based on body language. Without without realizing it, you can be communicating to someone that you are tough or off-limits.

There is no harm in asking for assistance if you feel stuck and don't know why your relationships aren't very successful. You might look for self-help books on the topic or consult with friends who seem to have a happy dating life. Your connection and interactions with everyone else in your life may be improved significantly by learning how to comprehend the other person.

Developing Relationships That Are Effective and Efficient

Relax after you've met your soul partner. Don't hurry your connection, please. On your first date, avoid broaching the subject of marriage or having kids. Try to avoid bringing up your ex in conversation. Keep in mind to be joyful and to share your joy with others. Don't obsess on previous relationships. Eliminate previous baggage. Don't carry your past relationships into a new one.

Attend to your partner. Learn about the individual. Examine your shared interests by talking about them.

All relationships are often seen as being very fragile and requiring additional work to preserve. A partnership, however, has the potential to be both secure and enduring despite several difficulties.

In a relationship, both parties must put in their fair amount of effort and strive toward a shared objective. It may function better if there is a positive connection between the two people, where collaboration and respect are evident. In this approach, everyone contributes to the relationship's success and moves closer to a shared objective. Relationships that are effective and efficient are the only way to achieve this.

Relationships work best when both partners are aware of your sentiments and point of view. Asking and listening to your partner about their wants can help you understand what is important to them. When your partner notices this, they will understand that you value them highly.

Open communication between partners about their thoughts and perspectives on all relationship-related issues is necessary for effective and efficient partnerships. It is not a good habit to assume that the other person understands our requirements and will provide assistance when we request it. For instance, one individual may place a high value on cleanliness while another may not. Each person has unique priorities, preferences, and dislikes. Make an effort to do the things that are important to your spouse if they are important to you. They ought to treat you the same way.

Relationships depend on mutual respect. Partners should respect one another in order to have a stronger connection. Simply listening to our partner and making a serious effort to comprehend how they operate might be enough to demonstrate respect. Do you pay attention to what your spouse is saying, or are you just awaiting your turn to speak? Develop your listening abilities.

Respect is the antithesis of making hasty decisions based on biased information and unsubstantiated facts. The basic core of a successful partnership is respect. Respecting both oneself and others entails doing this. Other people will respect and adore you if you do. Understanding one another requires active listening and the absence of preconceptions.

Dealing with your partner's differences head-on is a crucial component of creating a successful relationship. It's fascinating to see how individuals differ from one another. You could have two separate viewpoints in a dialogue when one person listens to the other person, for instance. Try to find a solution that benefits both parties.

When at least one partner recognizes the value of the connection, this is possible. Then, that individual would put up more time, effort, and energy to comprehend the demands of the other spouse. Even if you are unable to comprehend your partner's requirements, you should nevertheless make an effort to do so. Even while you may not think it matters, your spouse definitely does.

Informal conversations are good for building connections. They are at ease expressing problems and worries. They are also more at ease, which helps them think more clearly. creating a space where the other person feels comfortable expressing their emotions. The development of a successful relationship might be hampered by people's failure to communicate their thoughts and emotions. For everyone, relationships are crucial. In order to strengthen the connection even further, it is crucial to confront challenges and conflicts as soon as they arise.

While certain things are inherent, they should be regulated in all interactions and relationships. One is inherent in human nature. A history of stereotyping or distrust, blaming the other person for a difficult relationship, and ignoring the other person's emotions while concentrating on a task are a few more characteristics that may be seen in relationships. Having distinct and well-defined aims, duties, and expectations for each party in the partnership should be one of your goals.

WHY ARE ALL OF MY FRIENDS AGAINST YOU?

You ask the new man you're dating to spend the evening with your buddies on Saturday. You can tell your pals are going to like him since he is both handsome and educated. He engages everyone in discussion while enjoying a few drinks. When he departs after two hours, you inquire as to what they all thought of him.

They make an effort to be friendly, but it is obvious that he turned them off. They confess that he was rude and annoying after being persuaded to offer an honest assessment. You defend him by pointing out that he must have been anxious, and you then put their remarks in the back of your mind.

After a few months of dating, you even think about moving in with him. Slowly, you begin to understand what your friends were referring to, but you still want to disprove them and prove to the world that he is a wonderful individual. You learn via rumors that he has been having extramarital affairs shortly after telling him you love him. You break up with him and promise to take advice from your friends more often in the future.

You're more likely to leave the person and never look back if you see red signs on your own. When your friends tell you he's not the right man for you, it's tougher. Your natural reaction is to get defensive and disregard their criticism because you desire their praise. After months of grief and anguish, I've rejected friends' assessments of people I dated only to learn they were spot on.

It's challenging to be the buddy who must provide the unflinching reality. You might risk severing your relationship with them. They'll probably find their way back to you once they realize that you just wanted what was best for them.

I've been on a lot of first dates that immediately raised red flags, and I quickly removed them from my list of possible partners. If a person engages in any of them, avoid him at all costs. The same is true for you. Be prepared for the possibility that after doing one or more of the items on this list, a man won't contact you again.

typical warning signs on a first date

He arrives incredibly late and makes no attempt to explain or apologize.

He places your order without consulting you.

He spends the whole conversation talking about himself and doesn't seem to be curious about you.

You must talk to break the unpleasant quiet because he almost ever speaks at all.

He is continuously checking his phone and sending messages to others.

He lacks motivation for his unpleasant or hostile behavior.

He displays excessive passion and sobs to you about a personal issue.

You are so thoroughly bored with him that you keep looking at the time.

He doesn't care about keeping you secure.

He becomes very inebriated.

Embarrasses you, he.

He treats the waiter and other people on the street poorly.

He disparages his ex.

He expresses his hatred towards his family.

He has no opposing views and agrees with anything you say.

These are all broad warning signs, but you'll be able to tell on your date if he says or does anything dubious. It's crucial for you to take off your blinders and see him clearly since your buddies won't always be there to warn you. On a first date, he could attempt to disguise any warning signs in an effort to impress you, but soon his actual character will show.

Meeting Mr. Non-Incredible for a date

After weeks of Doug pleading with me, I eventually gave in. I had a couple meetings with him via acquaintances, and neither his appearance nor demeanor struck me. I nonetheless made the choice to give him a chance.

This date turned out to be the perfect example of how NOT to behave on a first date. Here is a rundown of what transpired:

He was an hour late arriving. I stepped outside as soon as he said he was there since he insisted on picking me up. He spent thirty minutes driving around the area in search of parking after blaming the traffic (which is usual for Los Angeles) for his delayed arrival. It didn't make sense why he parked at all since we had planned to travel for our date.

He had a terrible cold. I steer clear of ill folks since I'm a germophobe. He responded that he no longer had a fever and felt well enough for our date when I questioned why he hadn't cancelled if he were unwell. He coughed and sneezed the whole night, and I was horrified.

He had greasy, untidy hair and was dressed in ragged, outdated clothes. I was aware of his wealthy employment and the fact that he often wore a suit from prior interactions. He seemed to be making an effort to be as uninteresting as possible.

His automobile was a complete wreck. In the sweltering heat, we had to travel a mile to get to his automobile, which was the worst piece of trash I had ever seen. It was at least thirty years old, in disrepair, and had two smashed rear windows. He told me that his vehicle had an animal odor since a squirrel had built a home there. I smelt a combination of cannabis, vomit, and pee when I first entered, making me want to throw up. He said that the shattered windows would let the scent escape, but the fact that the air conditioner was also damaged just served to increase my disgust. I offered to drive and told him I would be happy to, but he refused.

Despite informing me in advance that he had our whole night planned, he had no ideas for our date. He approved of the concept when I proposed going to the Grove, a location featuring stores, eateries, and a theater.

He didn't want to utilize the fee-based parking lot, so he drove around in circles on side streets for twenty minutes until finding a place that was free.

I begged if we could go someplace to eat since I was famished. He didn't have a preference for what kind of cuisine, but when I mentioned several cafés and restaurants, he rejected all of my suggestions.

We decided on an Italian restaurant, and as soon as we sat down, he placed an order for appetizers without asking me whether I wanted them. A pitcher of beer was also ordered, with the instruction "one glass." He refused to let me place my own drink order.

He was pure unhappiness. In addition to coughing and sneezing, he lacked optimism. He never even tried to strike up a conversation, and he always wore a frown. I questioned him to get to know him, and he answered with a single word, not returning the inquiry.

He treated the waiter poorly. I made a special effort to be extremely kind and welcoming in an effort to make up for his rudeness, but the waiter was still unhappy.

After the menus were removed, he took out his phone and sat slumped over, staring at it until the meal arrived.

I stopped up trying to talk to him since it was like pulling teeth, so I just glared at the wall clock and wished for time to move more quickly.

He gorged himself. He threw it all into his mouth, letting sauce and food bits fly everywhere, while I gracefully chopped my meal into little pieces.

He requested a second pitcher of beer for himself, and by the time the dinner was through, he was thoroughly inebriated.

He discovered he forgot his wallet at home when the check came in. He agreed to pay me back on our subsequent date after I ordered the lunch. (Well, of course! No way was there going to be a second date.)

I wanted to cancel our awful date then and then, but I didn't want to drive with a drunk driver. I decided to see a romantic comedy since I had free tickets to the movie theater in that building.

We passed a group of dubious men as we made our way back to his vehicle. He was completely unaware of our surroundings and didn't quicken his speed at all, which made me nervous about what the men might do.

We returned to his vehicle in safety, and the journey home was quiet.

I strongly declined his invitation to visit my residence when he offered to do so.

He leaned in to kiss me as he drove up in front of my house. I hopped out of the vehicle and thanked you for dropping me off while pretending not to notice.

The lesson I learned was that everything about my encounter with Doug raised a red flag. I was astounded that one person could breach every dating guideline, but he did. I could have avoided an evening of warning signs if I had called it off as soon as I found out he was ill. Knowledge gained!

Swimming with women is not permitted.

I had a great time on my first date with Chris. He brought me to an ice cream shop, which is where I like to go on first dates, and we hit it off right away. We spent hours conversing, laughing, and edging closer to one another to feel out each other's energy since we had so much in common. He kissed me on the cheek and said me farewell at the conclusion of the evening.

When Chris said that he had been a swimmer in high school, I proposed that our second date take place at my local pool. We initially had a fascinating talk before going to our own rooms to get dressed. He came out wearing just a swimming suit and had an erection, so I knew he was interested in me. I looked aside, pretended not to see, and chuckled to myself.

We both dove into the water and had a great time splashing and flirting with one another. He mentioned in passing how he was forbidden from swimming with females when he was younger. He said that he was raised in a very religious family when I questioned him why. I inquired more, but Chris told me that he was no longer religious. I forced that truth from my thoughts as we switched to other issues.

The remainder of the date was fantastic! Swimming was followed by lunch and more bonding. We had a strong connection, and I was eager to find out all there was to know about him. Sadly, he was ready to go on a three-week trip to Michigan to see his parents. We said him farewell after having yet another great time and he made a vow to stay in contact.

Chris acted as promised. Without him, I was concerned that the three weeks would drag on, yet they went surprisingly quickly! Chris messaged me regularly, and we had long, deep discussions that went on all night. We told each other secrets and fears and life goals, and I felt like he was "the one."

Sadly, as soon as he got back in town, he disappeared from my life. I didn't understand what went wrong. I overanalyzed all our conversations and wondered what I said that could've pushed him away. I didn't sleep for weeks as I tried to come up with a logical explanation for his disappearance.

In most cases, when a guy ghosts me, I don't get the satisfaction of learning why. However, Chris popped back into my life a few years later. I had already moved out of state, but he sent me a long message apologizing for his behavior. He explained that his religious upbringing made him freak out about seeing me again. He was attracted to me but had zero experience with women. He assumed I'd want to be with a more experienced man, so he got scared and disappeared.

My takeaway: I appreciated his honesty, even though it was years later. I knew it took courage for him to admit that to me. I realized my mistake in pushing away his comment about being religious. It was a red flag that I ignored, but I should've paid attention to it. I assumed he had moved on from those beliefs, but you can't escape your past. It's a part of you, just like it was a part of him. Visiting his parents probably reinforced his religious beliefs, and he felt guilty for betraying them by swimming with me "in sin."

Summary

Don't ignore red flags or feedback from others. If you notice that something the guy says or does on your date makes you uncomfortable, get more information about it. If there are obvious red flags on your date, don't waste another second on him. And if you show any red flags, you shouldn't be surprised if you never hear from him again. Remember, it goes both ways.

Wants of Ideal Partners

Consider your ideal mate from their perspective. Given that they are someone you hold in such high regard, what qualities would they look for in a partner?

Read your list of characteristics that your perfect mate would possess again if necessary. Assuming you are that perfect person, make a list of the qualities you would look for in a relationship. Spend 5-10 minutes listing the qualities that your ideal partner—the person of your dreams—would value in a spouse. a person they would value and respect. Someone with whom they would be pleased to associate.

Now complete the task on the next page.

Step 5: Desires of Ideal Partners
List the qualities that you believe your ideal spouse would look for in a soul mate.

The ideal partner's don't wants (Step 6)

Consider what qualities your ideal partner would not desire in a spouse from the perspective of someone you hold in such high regard.

What are some examples of behaviors that a person you like and respect would not tolerate? What are the qualities and behaviors they look for in a partner? Spend 5-10 minutes thinking about possibilities, then attempt to circle the things you absolutely must not have.

Now complete the task on the next page.

Step 6: Things Your Ideal Partner Wouldn't Want

What qualities in a soul mate would your ideal spouse most certainly NOT want?

Seventh step: Compare your lists

Circle the positive and negative aspects of who you are or have when looking through the lists of your prospective companions.

Be truthful to yourself. Consider if you already are or might become the person your dream partner described. If so, you now have a map that shows both where you are and where you wish to go. When I mentioned that you can find your perfect partner by being wholly yourself, I really meant it. However, if you are aware of areas in your life that you can improve, it is your responsibility to do so. We weren't placed on Earth to perform the bare minimum. In order to live the greatest life possible, Tony Robbins refers to this as CANI, or continual and never-ending improvement.

Now complete the task on the next page.

Step 7 of the process: Compare your lists

This is a fantastic chance for you to develop and reach the level of person you know you need to be in order to draw the partner of your dreams. If you have lofty goals, you subconsciously understand that you also need to live there.

Which characteristics do you both share from your lists of what you bring to the table and what your ideal partner wants in a relationship?

What more items from your ideal partner's wish list might you fulfill if you could develop into the kind of person they desire?

Which traits do you both have from your lists of poor habits and your ideal partner's lists of traits they detest in their ideal partner?

Which one of them could you do without in your life?

We were sent on this planet to develop into the finest versions of ourselves.

That entails some duty on our part as individuals.

ARE YOU BEING WHO YOU REALLY ARE?

I mentioned this previously, and it really is astonishing how fast something like this can transform someone's life. I'm referring to the energies of the sexes. Both sexes possess the same energy. One is in charge, while the other is present only because of necessity.

There are certain guys whose genuine nature is masculine, and then there are other men whose true nature is feminine. Although it sometimes happens, a feminine guy does not always imply homosexuality. There are some women who are fundamentally feminine, and then there are those women who are fundamentally masculine.

Polar opposites are necessary to produce real polarity. Once again, polarity acts like two magnets that repel one another when held in the same direction. They are attracted to one another when you turn them over. We have polarity here.

If a woman is inherently feminine and is operating from a feminine state, she will always be drawn to a masculine man and repellent to a man who is not operating from his masculine state, sometimes known as a "nice guy". Now, in that stage, a feminine woman may date a feminine guy, but there won't be any passion. no desire for one another. Now, I'm not arguing that "nice guys" play the feminine part, but they do it more often than macho males.

Men experience the same thing. A macho guy who lives in a masculine environment will naturally be drawn to a feminine lady. They may have a relationship, but there wouldn't be that much passion if he ended up with a woman who is inherently macho or who is "just one of the guys," or "just one of the guys".

If they are living in their real nature, these pairings are necessary for polarity to function:

male and female are opposite genders.

masculine female - feminine male

feminine female - masculine female

masculine vs feminine

An excellent illustration of this is how, when you encounter a homosexual couple, you can typically tell which one is more feminine and which one is more masculine immediately away. Do you not concur? I'd want you to know that I don't mean to offend.

The way we spend our lives may affect how much this polarity idea explains. I'll explain. At this point, things become challenging. People's life may alter without them even realizing it.

Let's imagine that a guy doesn't receive much male time since his parents, who believe that all men are jerks, reared him. A fully masculine man may choose to live in his femininity in order to blend in with his surroundings, because he believes that being strong and harsh is a negative thing, or because he fears that the ladies in his life would not like him if he behaves too much like a boy. In order to avoid being terrible or being thought of negatively by the ones he loves, he may even alter his identity. People will go to great lengths to satisfy their demands. He could unwittingly dwell in his feminine form if being manly makes others hate him. I hope you can understand this.

Imagine a girl who is a daddy's girl. She fulfills his desire for a son. Even though it is not her natural condition, she will continue to be masculine in order to connect with her hero. I see so many young ladies who believe that acting like a little girl is wrong. They assert that a tomboy is who they really are. This normally corrects itself eventually, but not always.

Say a mother just become a single parent. She is now required to provide for the family, and she often adopts a male persona in order to step up and prepare meals. When something similar occurs, a woman often shifts into survival mode and unleashes her macho side. A single mother may spend years in this mode at a time and lose all memory of what it was like to be feminine and free. Can anybody else except me relate to this?

People are unaware that they are not living in their natural condition since all of these circumstances are subconscious, with the possible exception of a vague sense that something is wrong. A macho dude who has spent so much time in a feminine environment won't comprehend why that lovely feminine lady won't even give him a chance.

While I was writing this, I found it hilarious because I used to often get stood up in high school. I referred to myself as "just one of the guys" and the most of my pals were male. Why shouldn't they like me? I am a feminine lady who unwittingly spent the most of her life in a masculine condition. Perhaps for this reason, nobody outside of the "nice guys" was ever interested. Moment of clarity I'm just saying.

HOW TO DISCOVER TRUE LOVE AND LASTING JOY

According to the Law of Attraction, same behavior attracts similar behavior. You must thus really resemble the people you want to attract. This is because, as the saying goes, "You attract what you are, not what you desire."

You must first become real love in order to discover it. Make an effort to become the person you want to attract and associate with.

Love and accept yourself unconditionally if you want someone else to do the same for you. If you want someone to constantly be honest with you about their feelings, be honest with them as well. Be loyal if you desire a faithful partner. Although I could go on, I believe you get the idea. Be for others as you would have them treat you.

Every partnership serves as a mirror for self-reflection. This will help you determine if you are in or out of harmony with love. Love is the one Truth, the only God, and the only Reality, as was covered in the previous chapter.

Your thoughts and judgments about other people reveal realities about you. They serve as a reflection of how you are acting right now.

Your evaluations of other people show you where you need to improve on yourself. Exactly what you need to focus on to get rid of falsehood and accept Love is revealed by them. This holds true for how you feel in all of your relationships, including those with God, yourself, your family, friends, and loved ones, as well as with those you work with every day.

Not hatred, but fear is the antithesis of love. Fear is ignorance, which breeds hatred, and is the source of all bad or wicked. Fear (bad) is the shadow of Love (good); as Franklin D. Roosevelt famously observed, "The only thing we have to fear is fear itself." The shadows that light creates are only as real as the light itself, yet to people who live in their path, they seem to be extremely real.

Simply consider the term "EVIL." What further words may the letters form? Live, lie, and be evil. Evil is spelt LIVE in the same way as DEVIL is spelled LIVED. To live a falsehood is to live in reverse, against the truth.

Evil is a deception that hides the reality that Love is the only thing that exists. I'll say it again: God is Love, and God is the sole source of Truth. Evil is the vileness inside us that prefers to think, feel, and act from the perspective of our false master, fear, as opposed to the perspective of our genuine master, love.

Choosing love over fear in all of our ways is our constant battle.

Your true self is the one you keep concealed, the one you want people to know intimately and to adore without conditions. A soulmate connection is one in which you feel completely understood and loved and may be wholly yourself.

If you keep drawing emotionally unavailable partners, it may be a sign that you lack emotional openness and need to work on developing trust. If you attract people who are possessive and envious, it suggests that you are also possessive and envious and that you need to learn how to let go of attempting to control how things end out.

Whatever qualities you attribute to someone are qualities you possess as well. You must first alter yourself if you want to change what you attract.

Making your own reflection genuine is the key to finding your soul partner, loving yourself, and experiencing long-lasting happiness. This entails avoiding putting on any masks and refraining from trying to be someone else only to please them or win their affection. There should be no duality between who you are on the inside and who you appear to the outside.

You will never find your way home until you can let go of your desire for other people's approval and can love yourself enough to be your true self in front of everyone. Instead, since like activity attracts like action, you will continue to draw in learning opportunities and unreliable partners.

The Law of Attraction, also known as the Law of Love, serves to reveal who we really are and ultimately lead us to Divine Love via atonement.

Whether you are aware of this, agree with it, or believe it, every thought, word, action, and deed is subject to Real Love. Simply opening your eyes will allow you to see it. When you pause and take an honest look at yourself, it becomes clear that if you can't, you are blind.

Recognize what is right in front of you, and what is hidden from you will become apparent, said Jesus. Because nothing is kept secret that won't be revealed, according to the Gospel of Thomas.

Karma is about recognizing where our self-will is out of alignment with Divine Love's will (which is for us to love), and correcting it. (1 Peter 4:8) says that "love covers a multitude of sins."

If we have previously freely completed the self-work, which is aligning our will to the Divine Will, which is selfless love, love wipes out bad karma from the past that would otherwise need to come up with us later and teach us even tougher lessons because we resisted.

The individuals you are supposed to learn your most important life lessons from—about who you truly are and how you connect to yourself and the Creator (Divine Love)—are the ones who draw you the strongest.

These connections are intended to provoke self-reflection and the question "why?" They nearly usually make you feel the most anxious. They have an unmistakable physical allure, yet the one most involved frequently experiences a great deal of agony.

This is due to the fact that it is not a committed, evenly reciprocal love. You may wonder, "Why doesn't he or she love me back, or in the same way?" in unbalanced relationships. Why does loving this person sting so much?

Your soulmate is not the individual with whom you are in an unequally devoted and reciprocating relationship. This person is only intended to remain in your life for a limited time, until you have learnt your lesson from them about what True Love is and is not.

One will be far closer to finding their life mate, self-love, and happiness if they voluntarily choose to learn from, move beyond, and recover from these relationships rather of holding on and dragging them out for years. It will also make it happen even quicker.

FIGURE 4

After a long period in a toxic relationship with someone who never really cared about me, I was finally done and despised myself for it.Although it was painful, "i'm out" is the silver lining.

I commuted to work from a different leased apartment while remaining in the same city and seemed to be in my own place as I had always desired.

Sam was sincerely delighted for me and expressed how I now looked better at work and had eaten more than I had when he first met me. Because I felt comfortable confiding in Sam, I informed him about the current status of things and that I had moved out and in my own place as well. Since we both had the day off work on Saturday, he wanted to check out my new apartment. I was glad to have him stay with me since we always had things to chat about.

Sam arrived at lunchtime with a stunning dog and jingling, "You like him? You may keep him," I said as I opened the door to greet him. Startled, I swiftly grabbed the dog and struck him inside.

Sam was aware of my long-standing desire for a furry pet, a fact I had all but forgotten.

He revealed to me that he had been often visiting the animal shelter ever after I informed him I had moved into a new apartment and was staying alone. It eventually dawned on me that I could retain him now that I am no longer living with my ex-boyfriend. I was overjoyed. He had supper, we spoke and joked, and then he went. That evening, it was hard for me in some ways to say goodbye to Sam.

Monday was quickly approaching, and I couldn't wait to get to work and inform Sam about the recent changes in rookie's conduct. I made the decision to call my dog Rookie.

I had Rookie to keep me on my toes virtually every day, so I was a new me and had a terrific week. I realized I smiled more, found things thrilling, and things that had before been normal to me suddenly had a whole new, more intriguing aspect.

I loved being single because it made me feel liberated, strong, and youthful.

My life had also become less monotonous, and I wouldn't mind a little flirtation now and again. Most importantly, I always had something to occupy my time when Rookie and I were alone.

We would also take lengthy strolls, and while doing so, I would sometimes see some young, attractive males attempting to flirt with me. I improved my performance at work and learned to be more at ease with myself. I quickly received a promotion and realized that I had been placing myself in a box, believing I couldn't accomplish much more than what I was currently doing. It was truly lovely to get praise from others for a job well done.

I called my mother to update her on my accomplishments and to let her know that I had ended my relationship with my ex-boyfriend.

She didn't really like for the latter, but she encouraged me to laugh more as I had been doing from the beginning of our talk and shared my enjoyment with me. It dawned on me at that point that I had been laughing during the whole conversation.She seemed pleased for me and begged me to call her more often.

I didn't need to change anything about myself at this point because Sam and I were "two peas in a pod" when we returned to work. I looked forward to him telling his typical jokes about me and Rookies because they were always funny when he said them.

GETTING READY TO MEET YOUR SOUL MATCH

Do you place a lot of emphasis on the traits and characteristics you do want in your soul mate? Do you treat yourself the same way? The majority of the time, individuals seeking for a soul mate concentrate so much on what they want in a partner that they forget that the potential soul mate would also be wanting the same from them.

I was such a harsh critic, scrutinizing my possible soul mates to the nth degree. I inspected them as they arrived and went until I had found absolutely no soul match. I did anticipate them to be transparent, non-egoistic, polite, and modest. I was not very excellent at these same attributes, however.

Returning to My Soul partner Plan, I had outlined the "Things to Nurture" section with clarity since I knew it was the first step on my road map to meeting my soul partner. The following were my THINGS TO NURTURE in my plan:

1. Boost my sense of self

2. Be prepared to hear "no" as a response.

3. Concentrate on the nature of my soul partner

A healthy relationship always involves giving and receiving. You cannot expect anything in return for what you have not given. Do unto others as you would have done unto you, the Bible commands. We are also instructed to "love your neighbor as you love yourself" in the same Bible. These two statements have significant relational implications. Of course, there is never a 50/50 split in a relationship. Nevertheless, you must put out your best effort while allowing your spouse to do the same. The most important thing is to recognize that each partner is giving it their all.

How do you get ready to meet your soul mate? You must understand that you are the first step in performing your role. To find a compatible soul partner, you must be mentally prepared. Accept that you must rebrand yourself as a "sellable" commodity of love. Your soul mate should have no excuse to reject you because of who you are.

You must enhance your self-image if you want to repackage yourself as a "sellable" commodity of love. Yes, I did 'build up' my appearance to give the impression that I was a confident guy, but deep down, I was afraid of failure, commitment, being a husband, and finally, being a parent. It didn't take long for my beauty queens to get beyond my portrayal of a vapid self. So, it never took us this long to end our relationship.

I discovered this crucial truth via my own mistakes. I had already experienced what it was like to not be mentally prepared to be a soul mate before I made the decision that I needed to do so. I paid the fee, and I did it reluctantly.

Being mentally ready means realizing that you can no longer fully fulfill yourself without also satisfying others. You must now consider the other person who you hope will be your soul mate in addition to thinking about yourself. In order for someone else's soul to find a home inside you, you must let go of your fear of surrendering space. You must be willing to accept openness and free choice. Since clinched fists can not shake hands, you must extend your arms in order for the other person to feel really free to hug you. Everything starts with your psyche. Be honest and ready for everything!

You must remove the mask of your bad self-image, which is comprised of an ego that is prideful. I hid my genuine personality because I was afraid of being rejected, so I became a package that was only appropriate for beauty queens—a poisoned chalice!

Yes, I had to put my ego aside and have an open mind. I had to resist the inclination to manipulate my possible soul mates into submitting to my whims and wishes. I had to let go of the idea that by pinning a beauty queen to my bed, I was now royalty. Yes, I had to let my relationship with Agnes develop naturally, content with the opportunities it brought rather than attempting to push it down a predetermined course. It was all fun for me. We were only the content observers while our relationship meandered like a river, forming lovely patterns of life all the while.

In addition to mentally preparing yourself, create a mental map of the sort of future you want to pursue. Establish merely broad directions rather than established routes. Let the relationship choose its own course. Do not force your possible soul mate onto your mental map before letting him or her decide what is on theirs. Make a plan for your soul mate that will serve as a guide. And be prepared to discuss and make amends about the shared future you do want for your partnership when the moment is appropriate.

Avoid exploring too quickly and exhausting yourself before you reach the top. Finding your soul partner requires a long trip rather than a sprint. Spend some time getting to know, understand, and feel your possible soul partner. Although I had confidently included learning about "My soul mate's being" in My Soul Mate Plan, it is one such item that I gravely neglected to carry out. I was constantly in a hurry, expecting everything right now and placing expectations on others until my relationships with my beauty queens became so toxic that they just chose to end. I was about to do this to Agnes when I remembered My Soul Mate Plan. I'm happy I gained the realization I needed to turn around and go back on the correct path. You must constantly review your design as a sacred shrine in the refuge of souls to prevent such errors.

I was certain that Agnes embodied the kind of woman I would choose as my soul mate. Instead of rushing to express my sentiments to her, I waited for the clouds to gather from the myriad vapors of our happiness. Why the haste when I knew it would rain one day? While there was still sunlight, I did scatter hey. I relished the sunlight brought on by the rising sun of our radiant love.

Be the sort of person who gives prospective soul mates every reason to think you could be their match. Put your attention on developing yourself and rebranding yourself as that "sellable" product of love. Let rid of your inhibitions and be free to communicate with your soul mate. The first step to finding real love among free people is to set yourself free.

Avoid These People Like The Plague

if you had previously gone on dates. By this point, you would have obtained the required information, and the list below shows which individuals you need to steer clear of. But as much as you adore him, as I already said. People just get smarter; they don't change. Reduce your losses immediately. You must understand that neither you nor their goals are involved. They are who they are, after all.

Anything is possible if you have desire! This holds true for everyone. Several men and women strive to reach certain goals. will do everything and everything to succeed. if they sprang from nothing at all. Or it can be a result of their rivalry. Either you do things correctly or you don't. For instance, imagine hiring a guy to work on his career. Even though he doesn't have much, he still works. His present social circle is dictated by where he hails from. if he starts dating someone from a more exclusive social group. She wants him to achieve better, therefore she will undoubtedly assist him with his task. The ability to care for others is an innate MATERNAL woman attribute. Your DNA contains it. This individual will lie because he is always trying to improve himself and his network of friends. simply because his confidence has significantly increased. And more ladies are drawn to him. He has a better education. He dresses better than I do. His whole package has become much more alluring. He will discover that he is in circumstances that are unfamiliar to him. There is always a draw to new things.

Everyone is used to their present issues and how to solve them. if you find yourself faced with brand-new issues. You become more outgoing as a result. You can be loyal in your present situation. But with a new life comes a fresh mystery.

People who are fixated on money will lie. Anything they can do to increase their income! They don't care whether their actions do anybody harm. This also applies to women. They could sell themselves since the situation is so horrible and finally start escorting. But their objective was to marry a player. or a guy who has been kept. This is implied by the fact that they consistently purchase new items, even when they cannot afford them. They proudly display what they have and let everyone know about it! For these individuals, money is a sign of significance and power. The amusing part is that all you need to attract these con artists is money. They will regrettably depart you if you don't pay them.

Some males are not very chatty. Not everything I say! Others are quite silent. especially when confronted with a harsh environment. They are unwilling to discuss issues. They become much more quiet when they are not in charge. They turn around and leave after saying, "I need to digest what is happening and think about it." I'll contact you again. These youngsters are rumbling volcanoes that might erupt at any moment. They are waiting for a circumstance to arise so they can defend their behavior. They will claim that you didn't give me enough time to consider it or to speak. All defenses! They did, however, go someplace else. He is most likely vacillating in the relationship since he is unsure of his position. He is an ELEPHANT! When he becomes enraged, his whole existence gives him the go-ahead to cheat. His mind is in the right place! Children are prone to this behavior. Sadly, he has never developed beyond it or worked on it. These juvenile rants are ludicrous. As they won't ever want to speak to you about anything going on in their lives, you definitely do not want to be engaged with someone like them. They believe they are superior to you and have more knowledge. He'll probably spin around to face you and say. Where are currently not together I need a rest. You're planning your day's thoughts. He is considering switching to someone else for the day. He wants to go and sleep with someone else, but in truth, it's just a fight that's gotten out of hand or gone bad.

If you're dating someone and they demand a lot of your time and attention, they're probably going to cheat. It might be mental rather than physical. if you are not paying enough attention to them. It's gone! if they stare at the mirror nonstop. taking selfies and seeking your ongoing delight. Must command the spotlight. Let it be if the attention-seeking is how it all begins. Not worth the effort. Your life will be used as payment for his. These days, both men and women need a lot of care. This is a result of social media raising our self-awareness. You should have self-assurance and be aware of who you are.

Cheats will be caught. If someone brings up their history when you are out with them. They admitted that they had cheated in the past and felt bad about it. They have cheated before, therefore they will do it again. Since this is a brand-new relationship and offers them a second opportunity, they shouldn't inform you. When it comes to infidelity, men and women vary. Men engage in sex anytime it is presented to them. It thus boils down to convenience. Best think he is there if she is still alive. Even if he feels drawn to her, it is irrelevant. Although this seems horrifying, it is really extremely accurate. Women, on the other hand, will cheat on their relationship with someone better if they do. It is inappropriate in any case.

www.ingramcontent.com/pod-product-compliance
Lightning Source LLC
Chambersburg PA
CBHW050236120526
44590CB00016B/2105